Note to Parents

For many, the Seder night provides the foundation upon which they establish their view of what it means to be a Jew. Using the Haggadah as an instruction manual, each person is tasked with using the building blocks at their disposal to create their own educational masterpiece.

This Haggadah Companion began as a way to engage my children in the process of developing their Jewish identity through creativity, exploration, and collaboration. Brick by brick, year by year, this book took shape in line with their educational development and growth. It is my hope that this work provides a platform to build a solid structure upon which you find meaning and connection with the fundamentals of the Seder night.

Happy building!

Copyright © 2022 by Mosaica Press

ISBN: 978-1-952370-96-0

All scenes in this book were built by Tzachi Rosman using Lego bricks and photographed by Thomas Campos.

LEGO® is a trademark of the LEGO Group, which does not sponsor, authorize, or endorse this book.

All rights reserved. No part of this book may be used or reproduced or transmitted in any form or by any means, electronic or mechanical, including photocopying, recording, or by any information storage and retrieval system, without written permission from the publisher.

Published by Mosaica Press, Inc.
www.mosaicapress.com
info@mosaicapress.com

Kadesh, Urchatz, Karpas, Yachatz, Maggid, Rachtzah, Motzi Matzah, Maror, Korech, Shulchan Orech, Tzafun, Barech, Hallel, Nirtzah

קַדֵּשׁ, וּרְחַץ, כַּרְפַּס, יַחַץ, מַגִּיד, רָחְצָה, מוֹצִיא מַצָּה, מָרוֹר, כּוֹרֵךְ, שֻׁלְחָן עוֹרֵךְ, צָפוּן, בָּרֵךְ, הַלֵּל, נִרְצָה

קַדֵּשׁ
Kadesh

The Four Questions

מַה נִּשְׁתַּנָּה הַלַּיְלָה הַזֶּה מִכָּל הַלֵּילוֹת:

Why is this night different from all other nights?

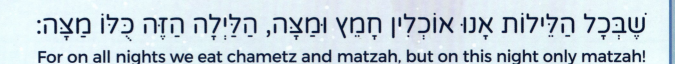

שֶׁבְּכָל הַלֵּילוֹת אָנוּ אוֹכְלִין חָמֵץ וּמַצָּה, הַלַּיְלָה הַזֶּה כֻּלּוֹ מַצָּה:

For on all nights we eat chametz and matzah, but on this night only matzah!

שֶׁבְּכָל הַלֵּילוֹת אָנוּ אוֹכְלִין שְׁאָר יְרָקוֹת, הַלַּיְלָה הַזֶּה מָרוֹר:

For on all nights we eat other vegetables, and on this night bitter herbs!

שֶׁבְּכָל הַלֵּילוֹת אֵין אָנוּ מַטְבִּילִין אֲפִילוּ פַּעַם אֶחָת, הַלַּיְלָה הַזֶּה שְׁתֵּי פְעָמִים:

For on all nights we do not dip our food even once, on this night we do it twice!

שֶׁבְּכָל הַלֵּילוֹת אָנוּ אוֹכְלִין בֵּין יוֹשְׁבִין וּבֵין מְסֻבִּין, הַלַּיְלָה הַזֶּה כֻּלָּנוּ מְסֻבִּין:

For on all nights we eat either sitting upright or reclining, and on this night we all recline!

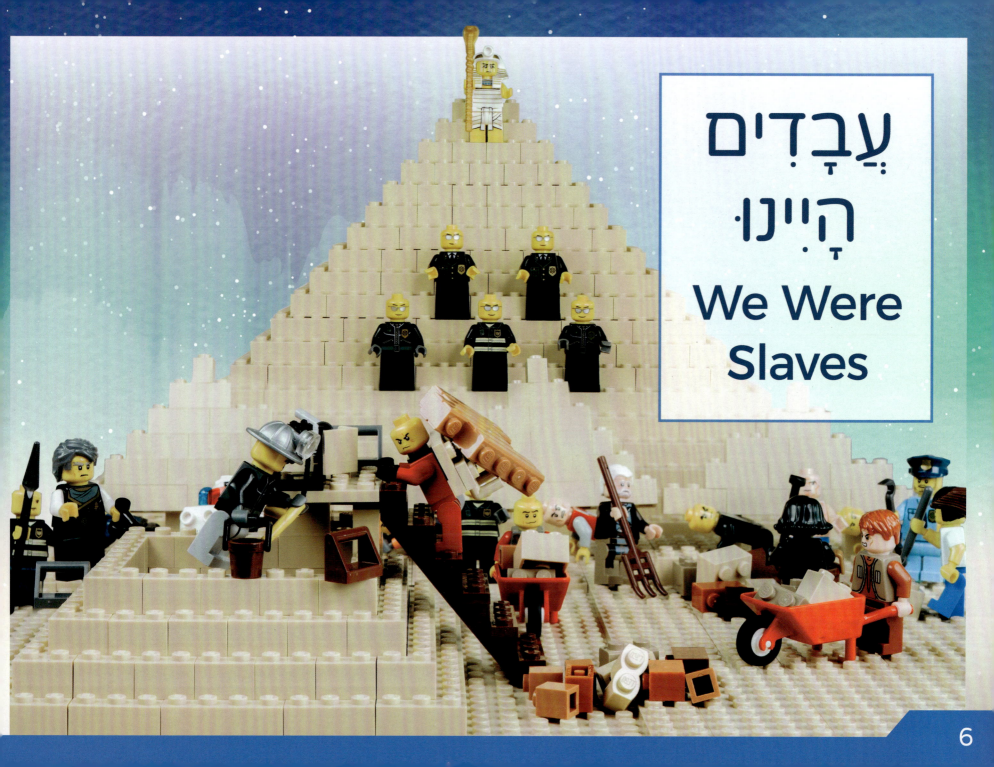

The Four Sons

חָכָם
The wise son

רָשָׁע
The wicked son

תָּם
The simple son

שֶׁאֵינוֹ יוֹדֵעַ לִשְׁאוֹל
The son who does not know enough to ask questions

Story of the Jews in Mitzrayim

The Jews multiplied and increased greatly.
(Exodus/שמות 1:7)

A new king arose over Mitzrayim who did not know Yosef.

(Exodus/שמות 1:8)

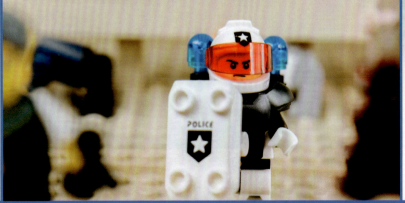

They set taskmasters over them to oppress them with forced labor.

(Exodus/שמות 1:11)

They made life bitter for them with harsh labor at mortar and bricks.

(Exodus/שמות 1:14)

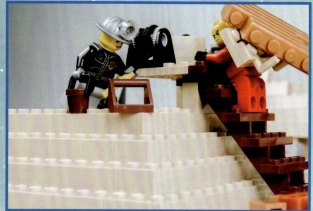

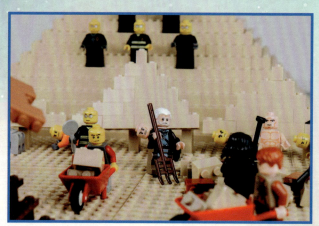

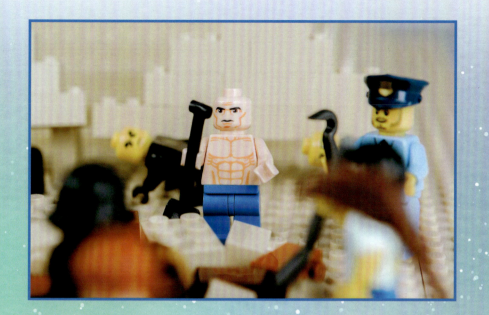

Sometime after that, when Moshe had grown up, he went out to his kinsfolk and witnessed their labors.

(Exodus/שמות 2:11)

The Jews were groaning under the bondage and cried out…to Hashem.

(Exodus/שמות 2:23)

Moshe and Aharon went to Paroh.

(Exodus/שמות 5:1)

The Ten Plagues

דָּם
Blood

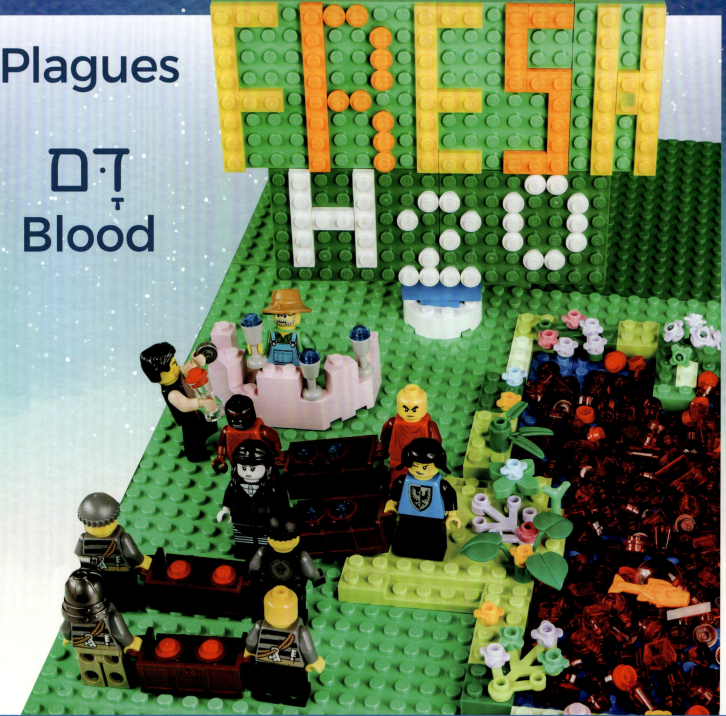

כִּנִּים

Lice

עָרוֹב
Wild Beasts

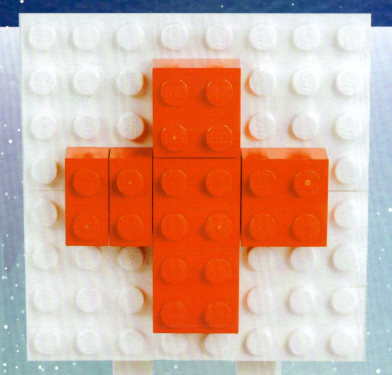

שְׁחִין
Boils

אַרְבֶּה
Locusts

מַכַּת בְּכוֹרוֹת
Plague of the Firstborn

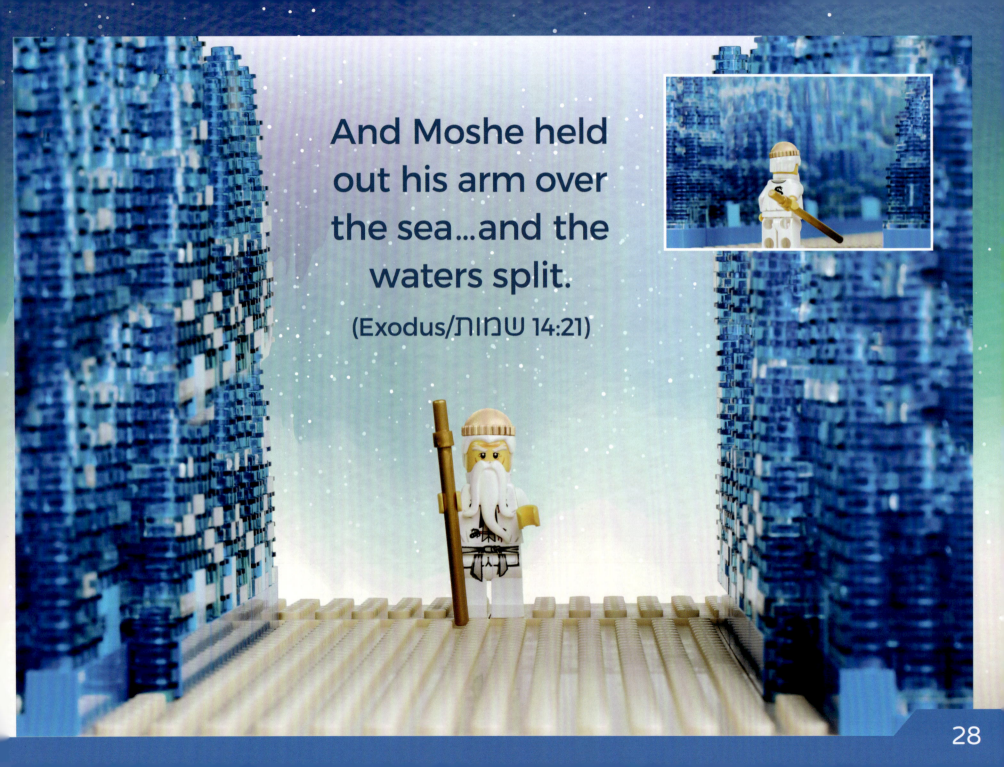

And Moshe held out his arm over the sea...and the waters split.
(Exodus/שמות 14:21)

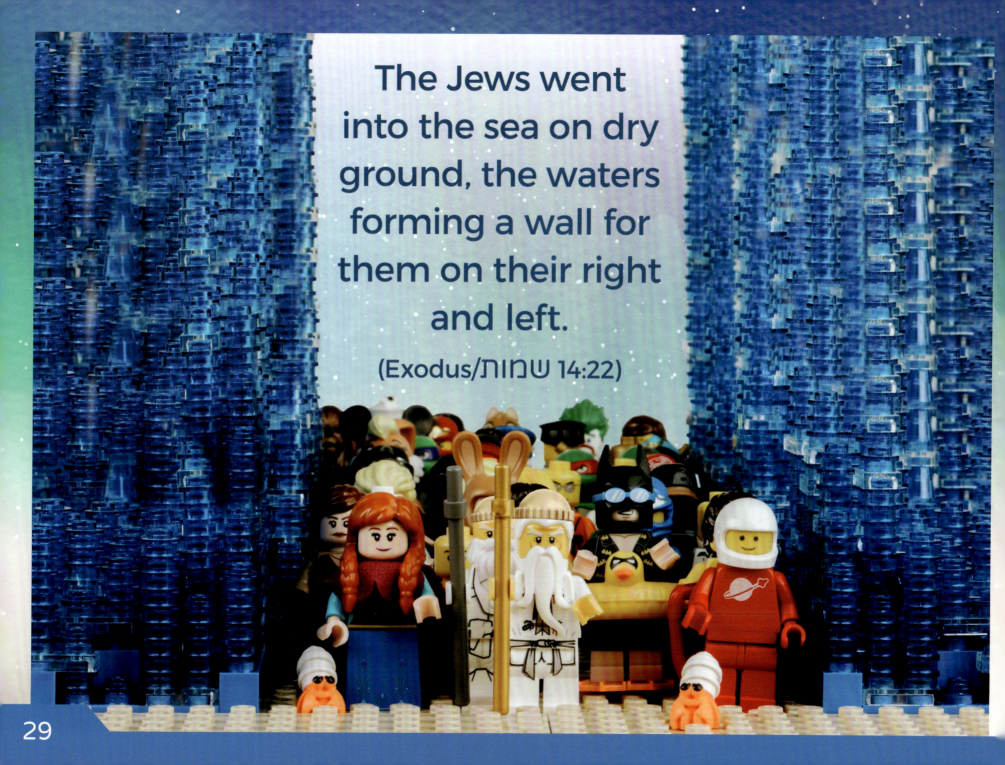

The Mitzrim came in pursuit after them into the sea, all of Paroh's horses, chariots, and horsemen.

(Exodus/שמות 14:23)

The Jews marched through the sea.
(Exodus/שמות 14:29)

The waters turned back and covered the chariots and the horsemen—Paroh's entire army.

(Exodus/שמות 14:28)

Then Miriam the prophetess, Aharon's sister, took a timbrel in her hand, and all the women went out after her in dance and with timbrels.

(Exodus/שמות 15:20)

מַצָּה
Matzah

פֶּסַח
Pesach

וּמָרוֹר
Maror

מָרוֹר
Maror

מוֹצִיא מַצָּה
Motzi Matzah

כּוֹרֵךְ
Korech

צָפוּן
Tzafun

הַלֵּל
Hallel

בָּרֵךְ
Barech

נִרְצָה
Nirtzah

Chad Gadya

חַד גַּדְיָא, חַד גַּדְיָא. דְּזַבִּין אַבָּא בִּתְרֵי זוּזֵי.

One 🐐, one 🐐—that my father bought for 🪙.

חַד גַּדְיָא, חַד גַּדְיָא.

וְאָתָא שׁוּנְרָא, וְאָכְלָה לְגַדְיָא, דְּזַבִּין אַבָּא בִּתְרֵי זוּזֵי.

Along came a 🐱 and ate the 🐐—that my father bought for 🪙.

חַד גַּדְיָא, חַד גַּדְיָא.

וְאָתָא כַלְבָּא, וְנָשַׁךְ לְשׁוּנְרָא, דְּאָכְלָה לְגַדְיָא, דְּזַבִּין אַבָּא בִּתְרֵי זוּזֵי.

Along came a 🐕 and bit the 🐱 that ate the 🐐—that my father bought for 🪙.

חַד גַּדְיָא, חַד גַּדְיָא.

וְאָתָא חוּטְרָא, וְהִכָּה לְכַלְבָּא, דְנָשַׁךְ לְשׁוּנְרָא, דְאָכְלָה לְגַדְיָא, דְזַבִּין אַבָּא בִּתְרֵי זוּזֵי.

Along came a 🪵 and hit the 🐕 that bit the 🐈 that ate the 🐐—that my father bought for 🪙.

חַד גַּדְיָא, חַד גַּדְיָא.

וְאָתָא נוּרָא, וְשָׂרַף לְחוּטְרָא, דְהִכָּה לְכַלְבָּא, דְנָשַׁךְ לְשׁוּנְרָא, דְאָכְלָה לְגַדְיָא, דְזַבִּין אַבָּא בִּתְרֵי זוּזֵי.

Along came a 🔥 and burnt the 🪵 that hit the 🐕 that bit the 🐈 that ate the 🐐— that my father bought for 🪙.

חַד גַּדְיָא, חַד גַּדְיָא.

וְאָתָא מַיָּא, וְכָבָה לְנוּרָא, דְשָׂרַף לְחוּטְרָא, דְהִכָּה לְכַלְבָּא, דְנָשַׁךְ לְשׁוּנְרָא, דְאָכְלָה לְגַדְיָא, דְזַבִּין אַבָּא בִּתְרֵי זוּזֵי.

Along came 🪣 and extinguished the 🔥 that burnt the 🪵 that hit the 🐕 that bit the 🐈 that ate the 🐐—that my father bought for 🪙.

חַד גַּדְיָא, חַד גַּדְיָא.

וְאָתָא תוֹרָא, וְשָׁתָה לְמַיָּא, דְּכָבָה לְנוּרָא, דְּשָׂרַף לְחוּטְרָא, דְּהִכָּה לְכַלְבָּא, דְּנָשַׁךְ לְשׁוּנְרָא, דְּאָכְלָה לְגַדְיָא, דְּזַבִּין אַבָּא בִּתְרֵי זוּזֵי.

Along came an 🐂 and drank the 🪣 that extinguished the 🔥 that burnt the 🪵 that hit the 🐕 that bit the 🐈 that ate the 🐐—that my father bought for 🪙.

חַד גַּדְיָא, חַד גַּדְיָא.

וְאָתָא הַשּׁוֹחֵט, וְשָׁחַט לְתוֹרָא, דְּשָׁתָה לְמַיָּא, דְּכָבָה לְנוּרָא, דְּשָׂרַף לְחוּטְרָא, דְּהִכָּה לְכַלְבָּא, דְּנָשַׁךְ לְשׁוּנְרָא, דְּאָכְלָה לְגַדְיָא, דְּזַבִּין אַבָּא בִּתְרֵי זוּזֵי.

Along came a 🗡️ and slaughtered the 🐂 that drank the 🪣 that extinguished the 🔥 that burnt the 🪵 that hit the 🐕 that bit the 🐈 that ate the 🐐—that my father bought for 🪙.

חַד גַּדְיָא, חַד גַּדְיָא.

וְאָתָא מַלְאַךְ הַמָּוֶת, וְשָׁחַט לְשׁוֹחֵט, דְּשָׁחַט לְתוֹרָא, דְּשָׁתָה לְמַיָּא, דְּכָבָה לְנוּרָא, דְּשָׂרַף לְחוּטְרָא, דְּהִכָּה לְכַלְבָּא, דְּנָשַׁךְ לְשׁוּנְרָא, דְּאָכְלָה לְגַדְיָא, דְּזַבִּין אַבָּא בִּתְרֵי זוּזֵי.

Along came the 🦸 and killed the 🗡️ who slaughtered the 🐂 that drank the 🪣 that extinguished the 🔥 that burnt the 🪵 that hit the 🐕 that bit the 🐈 that ate the 🐐—that my father bought for 🪙.

חַד גַּדְיָא, חַד גַּדְיָא.

וְאָתָא הַקָּדוֹשׁ בָּרוּךְ הוּא, וְשָׁחַט לְמַלְאַךְ הַמָּוֶת, דְּשָׁחַט לְשׁוֹחֵט, דְּשָׁחַט לְתוֹרָא, דְּשָׁתָה לְמַיָּא, דְּכָבָה לְנוּרָא, דְּשָׂרַף לְחוּטְרָא, דְּהִכָּה לְכַלְבָּא, דְּנָשַׁךְ לְשׁוּנְרָא, דְּאָכְלָה לְגַדְיָא, דְּזַבִּין אַבָּא בִּתְרֵי זוּזֵי.

Then 🔥 came and killed the 🦸 who killed the 🗡️ who slaughtered the 🐂 that drank the 🪣 that extinguished the 🔥 that burnt the 🪵 that hit the 🐕 that bit the 🐈 that ate the 🐐—that my father bought for 🪙.

חַד גַּדְיָא, חַד גַּדְיָא.

Glossary

Aharon: Aaron

Mitzrayim: Egypt

Mitzrim: Egyptians

Moshe: Moses

Paroh: Pharaoh

Yosef: Joseph